For Vanela & Jake
With gratitude,

Jonathan
Chacey

Surfing the Torrent

Surfing the Torrent

JONATHAN CHAVES

RESOURCE *Publications* · Eugene, Oregon

SURFING THE TORRENT

Resource Publications
An Imprint of Wipf and Stock Publishers
199 W. 8th Ave., Suite 3
Eugene, OR 97401

www.wipfandstock.com

PAPERBACK ISBN: 978-1-6667-8228-8
HARDCOVER ISBN: 978-1-6667-8229-5
EBOOK ISBN: 978-1-6667-8230-1

06/20/23

To Anna
for making me *happier than I ever
thought I would be*

Remarks

The Greek poems were all written in 1978, in Greece and in some cases shortly after returning to the USA. The poems in the second part date from various times in my life. In most of the more recent ones I have followed the example of Neo-Formal poets of today, writing in such forms as the sonnet, the villanelle, and generally with meter and rhyme, including one attempt at *terza rima*, although there are examples of blank verse as well.

The encouragement and support of Catharine Savage Brosman has been essential in my decision to attempt a book-length collection. I am a great admirer of her work, and I am grateful to her beyond words.

Some of these poems have appeared in *Ironwood, The Greenfield Review, The G.W. Review, Sino-Western Cultural Relations Journal, Chronicles: A Magazine of American Culture,* and *Academic Questions.*

Jonathan Chaves
Alexandria, Virginia
May, 2020

I

GREECE

1

Monemvasia

In the sunlight captured in her hair than which nothing
is brighter, more golden,
more like waves of silk,
I see impossibly white houses painted against flat cliffs
or blinding flashes of love on inconceivable waters.
In the darkness of her voice in anger
are hidden chambers covered with blue paintings
of sufferings and tortures or clarinets
in wild mourning for drowned swimmers and lost dances.
On the slopes of her body which I climb in ecstasy
are no trees but rocks softer than trees,
whiter, and which move in silent quakes
and when I reach the top, there is an empty church filled with ocean
    light
and mystery waiting for my arrival.
The paths to her soul never go straight
and must be traveled by donkey, they are so steep,
but keep stepping through the centuries,
under the archways inhabited by black-robed women grief-stricken,
joyous, weaving slowly the lace of the sky,
keep clip-clopping over the rough stones

past façades of chiseled sunlight
or little tables whose eyes never leave you
— the dark dregs in white cups, the hands like fields—
zigzag up the cliff-face, blinded, dazzled,
rise above the roofs of unimaginable white
— the flowers and the endless throbbing of the sea—
until you come at last to the windows of transparent stone
bathed in light, light air— blue, white, yellow—
the ancient castle, the home of dreams and waking from dreams—
Wake up, you have arrived, she is waiting for you,
drink a toast to her with the wine of the air,
you love her more than anything. . . .

2

Corner Table

Perhaps it was like this for you,
here, walking down this street,
in the bland warmth of the early afternoon.
Of course you didn't feel that you were in a foreign country.
You saw the green sunlight under the trees where the children played
and wondered if a secret message of love would fall from one of
    the balconies.
It was early August, and something
—maybe the way a baby cried in the square ahead—
told you that you would leave someday
and not come back for years.
The chairs before the sweet shop—four to each round table—
were still empty, as fresh as brushed teeth,
except for two foreigners sharing a bottle of Amstel beer at the corner.
but you did not notice them.
If you could have stopped and looked,
you might have seen the man in the message from the balcony,
sitting with a woman much like yourself,
but happier than you ever thought you would be. . . .

3

Gyzi

Do you remember the day of the tomatoes,
how they took us unawares
as we walked the neighborhood street in Athens,
and happened to glance to the right,
downhill on one of those side-streets in Gyzi
that seem so bland and so eternal:
dazzling, piled neatly in the merchants' carts,
orange, the orange of komboloy beads
that seem to glow from within,
the way the sun should surely look
if it were not so remote and so intimidating,
if it were something you could expect to eat,
truly the fruit of the earth,
yet here in the heart of the city,
glowing like the heart of the street below,
and of course we turned and followed that wonder
to find the Wednesday market overflowing
along the next parallel street down the hill—
not only tomatoes, but squash, eggplant, and the shouts
of the merchants as they competed
for the attention of the shoppers,

trying to be heard above the wild island music
played by a cassette recorder with double speakers
which a beggar carried down the center of the street
outspread for all to hear as if he were carrying the Torah.
I forget where we were going that day
— I know we got there, and finished what we set out to do—
but it is the tomatoes I remember,
that miraculous vision seen
as we walked unexpecting
towards some premeditated goal. . . .

4

Women and Fishermen

Beautiful Greek women,
you walk in pride and suffering
along the Athenian avenues
and your men carry rosaries,
each bead a circle of colorful earth.
Olives, stars after rain,
each is a sip of wine from the barrel
sending its tendrils
—soft, tenacious—
deep into the soul.
Olive tones of the paint on the martyr's face,
the twist of his head back, back in suffering,
the lines, the lines weighted with pain
as the fisherman's line is weighted with hook and bait.
Beautiful fishermen of Greece, what do you fish for?
Haul in your nets, strung with weights and floats
like beads on rosaries,
gather in the stars, the olives,
and every martyr,
fishermen of our souls. . . .

5

Transformation

If I were in this play
my clothes would glow like church windows
or summer trees—
the light would shine through my leaves,
on the children playing below.
I would carry my sufferings
in a hump on my back
as I trudged good-naturedly through the desert.
My arm would be long and quintuple-jointed,
making it easy to steal food
but hard to cause real pain
if I struck a child for a wrong answer.
My ancestors might be Chinese—
one of them could transform himself
into an animal, an insect or a snake.
I would speak in metaphors,
I would always be hungry,
I would give some people my dirty feet to kiss,
if I were one of these leather figures,
these shadow-puppets on the screen. . . .

6

Ocean and Olives

The forgotten lives
sacrificed to each olive tree
approach the ocean,
the hour of their return
marked by a rock
like a sundial in the water.
And we bake in the sun
like loaves of village bread.
A memory of silent warriors
with helmets and shields
glides behind the peninsula.
They sail to battle
in a boat the color of dried blood,
the red of sea animals
that cling to the rocks.
Ladders lean against the olive trees—
the trunks, twisted memories of pain,
are impossible to climb.
In the shade, a fingernail slits
the young green olive,
releasing its fresh odor,

a promise
which could never be broken. . . .

7

Milopotamos

Let us descend into this flower
its petals are the air around us
the path down is twisting, even treacherous
but surely we approach the fragrant receptacle
our bodies lighter with each step
the heat so intense that everything burns transparent
and a coolness awaits us
beyond the tiny pebbles of white pollen.
As we continue down, the green leaves embrace us
and the bright brown walls with their hidden caves,
and we pass through them to the edge of the waters,
this diaphanous jade!
Now we are fish of the heart,
fish of the flower,
floating with no purpose
in the wineglass of the sun.

8

Journey by Air and Water

The fish swimming high in the water
peers down at the rocks
watching for plants to graze upon
like a sheep.
And your raised arms in the photo of yourself
as a young girl reciting a poem for smiling faces
—thin moustaches and finely done hair—
you were swimming where none of them could follow.
The woman with the face like the sun
says some of her daughters have dried up on land,
but others flourish at sea.
They are casting yellow nets that breathe water gently,
then dry in the sun, and return to the ocean—
the ocean which is like a sky
where fish land like birds among rocks,
these hidden mountains
rediscovered millions of times. . . .

9

Landscape of Thought

The fisherman's wife,
standing in the grey fishing boat
as it leaves the harbor,
holding the yellow scarf
tight on her hair
so the breeze won't blow it away—
we will never know what she is thinking.
Is she thinking of the ocean, or the mountains,
the ocean which accepts the kisses
of her boat,
the mountains which are almost blue?
Is she thinking of both?
Or are her thoughts like those outlines
of mountains drawn in sand
by ocean foam
as it reaches its highest limit on the beach,
its final exhalation of salty breath,
and then rests,
accepts the pull of ocean behind it,
returns to its origin in the depths
among the fish and squid?

Those mountains last for seconds of time,
and then are replaced by new ones,
different ranges of sandy particles,
always forming the same landscape.
Perhaps it is this landscape she enters now
alone with her husband
and her thoughts.

10

To a Woman Who is a Fountain

You are a fish in the water
and the water itself.
Those who drink from your fountains
cast aside their crutches
or hang them on the wall.
You are a windmill
drawing the water of life
from hidden wells,
an oven baking loaves of wedding bread
on which are molded flowers,
grapes, and fish.
Those who enter your doors
burn candles and incense
which smells of trees in canyons,
and they remember
descending into the canyon,
through the pink flowers
to the stream below,
flowing with water so pure
it seemed almost invisible. . . .

11

An Island

I want to live in a country
of tiny white churches
perched like wild goats on rocky peaks,
churches which sing
pale blue songs to the ocean,
a country whose men
wear moustaches that sweep up in pride
like the horns of bulls
or the flight of ecstatic dreams,
where the arms of the mother
open across the horizon
to accept each child
as the harbor accepts the journeying ship,
where each man and each woman
enters daily into tiny churches—
with racks of wine barrels
for altar screens
and kitchens for altars—
a country whose ancient ancestors
built cities without walls
and painted their homes with frescoes

which now adorn the smokestacks
of their ships at sea,
whose old women walk
in procession into the sea,
hold hands in the shallow water
and laugh as they slowly dance,
a country shaped like a boat or a fish,
asail in the ocean for thousands of years,
whose air is perfumed
with incense and oregano,
whose mountains are crevassed
with sensuous canyons,
loved by its people,
people who want to live
as much as the people of my country
seem to want to die. . . .

12

Lassithi—for Anna's birthday

Imagine you are a valley
and your years are windmills—
you grow more beautiful
with each cluster of white sails,
giant chrysanthemums
twirling silently in the wind.
Women with white head cloths
walk your paths—
they too grow wiser with the years.
Mules, goats and cows
graze in your fields
beside the potatoes—
Summer is your season of greatest beauty,
when apples shine on your trees.
Gods are born in the caves of your mountains
and your sons and daughters
leave for distant countries,
but they know they must return,
to you, to you,
always to you,
and when they come back,

you offer them salads
from your gardens
and bouquets of windmills
like white flowers
which will always perfume their years.

13

At the Village of Fountains

The mountain behind the clouds
laments for the grey stones.
The stones—
slabs on the roof of the church—
remember a baptism nineteen years ago.
They are lined with cracks
like wrinkles on the face
of an old woman.
The woman laments
beneath the mountain.
She is the grandmother of a boy
whose blood has stopped flowing
after nineteen years.
Water flows beside the street
carrying with it sticks
thrown by children,
shadows of grey clouds,
and the woman's voice—
a spring rising from a crevasse in her heart. . . .

14

A Festival

First the mountains called us
and we came to them—
entering the dream
of a flock of sheep
as they slept beneath a tree.
The voices of their bells
reached us over fences of white stones.
Then we were called by the clarinets
and we came to them,
and we listened to their wild music
as we ate pieces of grilled meat.
This day was the festival of the sheep:
we worshipped them with our bodies
and with our souls.

15

Olga's House

If you enter the house
of the woman in black
you will see black everywhere.
The beds and couches
are covered with black cloth,
black cloth hangs in every window.
The air beneath the three arches
of the living room
is heavy with the blackness
of death.
Photographs of the one who has died
are in every room, all in black
and white.
And through the rooms passes the shrill voice
of lamentation
leaning on a cane
as it climbs the stones
of its winding path. . . .

16

Zagoria

Many things are hidden
in these mountains:
the sheep are known
only by the ringing of their bells,
softer even than the wind in the trees
which hide them;
wild highwaymen
hide in the caves
which dot the walls of the canyons,
and the canyons
are great secrets
kept by the mountains
for millennia.
Nomads move with the seasons,
carrying chickens and furniture
on their horses,
but only the ringing of their bells
is heard as they pass by night.
The villages hide
as the salamander hides on the rock—
the houses of grey stone

sleep on the ridges
like sheep which have turned to stone.
Stillborn children were once hung
over the fire and smoked for forty days.
Living grandchildren still remember.
After forty days, it stops raining.
The first man in a new world
finds himself standing beside a rough wooden cross
with mountains in all four directions. . . .

17

Milies

The frog is on guard forever—
bow down to him,
as did the ancient king.
His is the kingdom of flowers,
a different color with each step!
And the red flowerpots
which climb the stairs
towards a sky of brilliant swallows.
And there are the ants—
no dream beneath the roots!—
working in two streams,
gathering bits of straw
and dragging them over the stones
of the winding street
to their hidden kingdom forever.
And between slabs of stone
the fruit of the mountain overflows,
streams of water from hidden sources
along the streets and across the streets
of this village.
On the roofs of stone,

darkness sleeps
in vast jars like caves.
In a church with no roof
the rooster crows from an icon of blue sky.
And in a church which is like a cave
the priest in his dark vestments
lights incense and rings the bell
of attentiveness:
Remember the saint with the head of a dog,
the anguished skeleton
in the open coffin! . . .

18

Behind the Wall

At last we have looked
behind the white wall
on the mountainside,
encircling the grove of cypress trees,
and we have found this village
for the dead,
whitewashed tombs
with painted trim
like houses along a winding street.
Oil lamps burn on the roofs,
women change the flowers
and talk about the dead.
The dead speak to us,
asking us to weep at their stories,
and their words are poems,
written in couplets
and enshrined in tiny altars
behind glass.
Beside each altar,
two brightly painted vases
stand like a pair of birds or souls:

one faces the cross, the other turns away
and gazes down the mountain
where the shepherd brings home his sheep,
three hundred—
each with black markings
like fingers on its face.
The shepherd is seventy-three.
Tonight he will walk
with his wife into the village,
past the shops and whitewashed houses
to the blue doorway of his home. . . .

19

Rough Ocean

My soul could be this seagull,
fighting the wind, or this boat
with its red anchor
like a heart,
in harbor today because it is too windy
for fishing.

When these winds die down
the boat will move out
into the open sea
and the fishermen, cigarettes dangling from
their mouths,
will cast their nets into the ocean—
and with them, thoughts
of sad eyes behind half-opened doors at home;
Perhaps their souls
are the fish they will catch.

20

Kandia

Soon we will be a silhouette
on the horizon,
a ship in the dreams
of those left on shore,
and as they dream of us,
waking they will enter our dreams
dressed in black
with eyes as blue as this sea.
They lament our departure
as they celebrate our joy,
and we remember their faces,
their hands,
and their voices,
their voices which cry with a music
no mountains can contain,
though the bones of their grief
are exposed in hidden caves.
Now, as we leave their island,
approaching the horizon,
birds follow our ship
like memories of us

or dreams
as we become a kind of vision. . . .

21

The Color of the Ocean Last Summer

Some things cannot be remembered—
one of them is the color of the ocean
last summer
or even yesterday.

The brilliance in memory turns to darkness, the sharp
blue of the edges of the waves
becomes the dull blade
of a ceremonial dagger
worn a century ago.

The coolness which makes us gasp
in its gentle embrace,
the blue wind,
the loving arm of the harbor
and its fishing boats—
all become something like the sound
of a door closing somewhere
in a deserted mansion.

A man hears this sound in the distance—
the blue, the brilliance,
the arm of the harbor—
and he paints a picture
which hangs in a gallery
few ever visit,

and even the painting is hard to remember.

22

To the Master of Ships

These ships are muscles of color,
a joy pulled up on the strand,
tough links of earth, sea, sky
hauled in by sailors in white,
four tiny men to a pulley,
four pulleys—and a huge red chain.
Old man, eighty-two years old,
your eyes are dazzling,
blue which is the sun,
red the anchors to the green
of this earth—and white
bunched on the masts, folded wings
of gulls flying soon to follow
the breasts and curling tail of the angelic mermaid:
she holds a red anchor in one hand
and blows a trumpet call of fearless joy
to the waves, to the gentle
breaking of their foam, pulled in again
by your life-giving blue,
Christopoulos! On your last journey
may your ship reach the Heavenly shore.

23

Remembering Gianni

IN MEMORIAM GIANNI CARAVELI

There is less love in Athens now,
a grove of trees will be thirstier than before,
the soil they are rooted in will crumble,
and visitors to the coffee shop across the street
as they sip their lemon sodas
will see only a dusty plot of land,
gaping and vague, beyond a wire fence.
The eyes which knew each twist of each trunk
are crumbling, and in them reflections
of trees, vines on wire fences,
and clay tiles on old roofs.

A kind of beauty has died, something fine and subtle,
like a tiny wisp of cloud in a perfect sky,
or a sip of dry red wine from the barrel.

Across the mountains of this summer,
waves approach the beach where old men are taking
their last swim beside their children and grandchildren.
They float motionlessly, as if sitting in great armchairs,
soaking in every drop of light.

****

II

Journey and Destination

The Patriarch

—FOR STEVE ADDISS

I think his soul still flies here
a black bird or words
that curl or leap or fly,
soaring above all obstacles—
the false longings
the spit in the face—
though he never moves
from his place;
and the cane, the staff
that brought him here
pierces the words of his life story.

Three Sonnets on Memory

FOR STEVE ADDISS; A 70TH BIRTHDAY PRESENT, WITH FOND MEMORIES OF JOHN M. CRAWFORD, JR.

1.

Memory sees two men in two chairs,
As it peers back—or does it peer ahead?—
A conversation that one thought was fled
From presence now continues unawares.
One's dress is all conservative, his hairs
Are closely cropped; his shoes are leather, black;
The other's hairdo cascades down his back,
Exotic bloom adorns the shirt he wears.
Chinese art surrounds them—jars and screens—
And these seem brought to life by what they say;
Memory is deaf, and has no means
For capturing their words!—But let us pray
That sound, uncaptured, flutters and careens
All disembodied, 'til the final day.

2.

Their conversation—what was thought and spoken—
Word alone, pure soul, and lacking flesh,
Is yearning for a body to enmesh
Its strivings somewhere living, then, unbroken,
Ideals may prove to be more than a token
Of final goals towards which each man does push;
We get there slowly, never in a rush,
Then all, we hope, is new as we're awoken.
Will they awake, these men, these gentle chatters
On Chinese art, or will they remain here,
Inside this picture? Yes, I think it matters—
Their fate links to our single greatest fear,
The fear of death, that everything gone scatters
Into the Void, leaves nothing, not one tear. . . .

3.

"The Void? That doesn't sound so bad!" you cry,
"It sounds all free, all unrestricted!" Still,
Our two men wish to walk on land, to feel
The breeze upon their brows, as they climb high.
They want the Chinese jars and screens still by
Their sides, and when their talking's done, a meal
That tastes and feels good! They wonder—will
Such yearnings be fulfilled? Will earth and sky
Be all transformed, all different, yet the same,
Just as we know them, but perfected? Why
Should they not be? We sense that the end-game
Takes curing: World, you do your best, you try

To run but cannot, since both feet are lame.
A time may come when you can even fly!

29

Two Poems on Marriage

1. THE SONG

I cut my finger
on the edge of your dreams. The blood flowed
indistinguishable from the tomato sauce or was it
ketchup for potatoes.
I pouted like a child, refused to kiss
the sensual hand proffered to me by
each moment— a child bearing a candle.
I am a child who cannot dream or can
only dream— This is what you have
taught me. Now the women of the ages
sing to me and violins of violent
mourning, clarinets of discipline sing to
me. I try a few steps of a dance, or read
some lines by Ritsos.
Each word is a thistle:
Gamos, Gamos—
This is what you have taught me.
The wine mounts, Oh, take me away, let me weep

like these clarinets:
"My beloved friend, your clarinet!"
Marry me to the earth, the black trees,
the canyons of white stone,
the village streets which breathe like mountains,
yes, yes, the song which you have taught me
is the song I wish to sing!

2. WANDERER

The sun shone too brilliantly, flattening
everything to the whitewash of joy. Now the
earth calls for rain again, and it falls. You have
left our wedding to attend another altar; music
plays there, with undertones of darkness.
Looking from me you stand at the window—
outside, a ship, with a mast shaped like a cross.
But this you do not see. Your eyes seem fixed
on something beyond or within. If you would
turn to me, night's mists would rise from the
mountains and the evergreens. Until then,
wanderer, if they bind you to that mast, make
sure the ropes will loosen and fall in time: here,
in this Ithaca of ours,
I will be awaiting your return.

Welcome Back to the Season of Dripping Trees

—INSPIRED BY A PAINTING OF HO HUAI-SHUO

I try to give off my own light
like a tiny white house
                    with a red roof
in the clearing of an endless forest.
The moist branches, thick and black,
Or sparse and brown,
Twist in primal, delicate patterns.
Some thrust straight at the sky, or gesture lightly
towards the ground;
each movement trails off in space.
One afternoon in Athens, the rain
Seemed to bring new life after so many days
Of unremitting brilliance. The acropolis swam
In cloud, and frogs croaked above the graves Of proud,
bearded men, and ladies
Who wore sandals and peered in jewel boxes. White
birds, tiny hearts of light, Perched at the tips of the
cypress trees.
Now that day is less than a dream;
There is only the somber beauty of denial.

The Girl on the Orange Line

Mysterious, the ways of God, and fine
The wonders He performs! No plans prepare
For knowing who may be just standing there—
The girl on the Orange Line.

On way to work, the sun not out to shine,
The platform gray, the Metro train so slow,
I glimpsed beside me one I did not know,
The girl on the Orange Line.

There was no omen, nothing like a sign,
But in her face I somehow felt I could
See faintly glimmering something deep and good,
The girl on the Orange Line.

She had an iPod, just like one that's mine,
Was listening to music, and was waiting
Like all of us—it really was frustrating!—
The girl on the Orange Line.

I had to be at work that day at nine;
I broke the silence: "Where's the train?" And she
Took off her headphones, and just smiled at me:
The girl on the Orange Line.

I did not wish to bellyache or whine,
Nor had I any carefully laid plan,
There was no goal in what I then began—
The girl on the Orange Line

Just seemed a moment's lovely anodyne;
I asked, "Have you a button that might bring
The Metro quick?" Her laughter bright did ring,
The girl on the Orange Line.

What happened next? I did not fall supine,
I did not fall in love at all, and yet
This much I know: I never shall forget
The girl on the Orange Line.

Three Birds

for Anna on her Birthday

JULY 1 2018

The Pelican has fed her children
With her own blood— She has
Pierced her breast
In anguished love
For them
And as the last drop falls She dies.

She returns to life
As a tiny woman
Lying spread-eagled
In a nest
High on a tree branch
Praying for protection—
A vast wing shadows her,
Spread by the Phoenix. She
Will grow again.

She hears a song of passion,
Of dazzling colors,
A brilliant Parrot,
Mexican, Portuguese,
Pointing a blood-red wing
Towards the merging of ocean and horizon
Where all is blue:
She gazes there— She has
Been there— She wishes
To return.

Rosemont Manor

... And then the flames intensest glow
When far off watchers think they die.

—PATMORE, "THE ANGEL IN THE HOUSE"

Climb the steps that lead to Rosemont Manor;
View the owl perching just above.
He's stood for death, he's also stood for wisdom;
He's never, in my knowledge, stood for love.

This house however was a gift from someone
Unto his bride in eighteen hundred eleven.
We cannot read the soul, but surely they
Aimed for life together, then for Heaven.

Maybe he reminds all those who marry
On these majestic grounds that they'd be wise
Each to sacrifice unto the other
Part or all if they would win the prize.

For three days now we've lived beneath this portal
Leading to a domesticity
Patmore called for, and we two have tried for
Blessed to be together, fervently.

A Wall Painting

Do not think that they hold no blood
these bodies of the saints
their robes have soaring melodies
for folds
they are dark pink, gold
and blue, yes—
their faces have auras like platters of gold
and they do look up
towards a city of domes
and parapets.
But they are martyrs
underneath,
vulnerable bodies
crowned with blood,
hands raised in a motion
of complete
resignation of soul
to body, body to soul
eyes brilliant with dark absence—
the fellowship of death.
They sway in place
pressed against each other—
and await
the final merging with God.

Remembering Frost

It must have been in '58 or so:
I 15, and Frost at 84.
The Breadloaf Writers Conference—I just know
My first and maybe only time to soar

Towards Mount Parnassus in the presence of
A poet, "swinger of birches," who was one
Of the chosen as I knew through love,
A man who rose before me as the sun.

An old man to be sure, his cheeks all furrowed
As is the soil of New Hampshire and Vermont,
Tracks not of the mole who's slowly burrowed
In Tartarean darkness, but a fount

Of Green Mountain water springing chill
From that soil, ranging towards the lake
Where my youth touched, for better or for ill,
First dream of the Beyond for Beauty's sake.

As I roamed those pathways, now alone,
Now with friends I could not yet embrace,
I resonated with the wondrous tone
Of what he wrote, he of the poets' race.

Later I grew older and I confess
Read academic critics who found wit
Where I had missed it, rendering him less:
Cleverness no match for soul. I sit

Today in quarantine and still can look
Towards his face smiling slightly when a friend
Asked for "Mending Wall"—he opened book,
And read two lines, then closed it: "Why pretend?"

He chuckled, then continued, voice quite hoarse,
To recite the whole from memory;
There was nothing false there, nothing coarse,
But there was light that everyone could see.

Simplicity? Complexity? These twain
Are weighed in balance, and the former held
Inferior to the latter. But in vain:
God is Simple—Legion hath rebelled.

To the Memory of Arthur Waley

It was in youth I first read your *Translations*
From the Chinese—perhaps I was fourteen, Or fifteen—
this the first of many stations
That led me from Vermont's fair mountains green
To mountains of the mind. Straight to my heart
The poets spoke, they caught the wondrous sheen
Of what surrounded me, they stood apart
From all the dusty world, and found a peace
Where I too found it, or had made a start.
No teachers there, no parents, no police,
But only friends who spoke across the years
And miles to join old China to old Greece.
They soon became my brothers, and the tears
They wept I wept and laughed with them as well;
They were to me as soul-mates and as seers.
If your work had not been there, I would dwell In quite a
different world today, what's more
It might have been no heaven, but a hell:
And you, my friend, first opened up the door.

Acrostic Eulogy for Burton Watson

Before Burt Watson, glimmerings of light
Unfurled their banners on the murky deep,
Reflected from the waters unexplored
That spread before us—ancient Chinese culture,
Ocean still awaiting galleons,
Not yet penetrated to the farthest shore.
When Watson put his hand to pen and paper,
At last the darkness lifted from the sea,
Thus mapping channels that might guide our ships
Straight towards the harbor at the far horizon
Of China's treasured past, her deepest heart
Never yet revealed with such full clarity.
Basic Writings: *Chuang Tzu, Han Fei Tzu*—
Untranslated, or badly done before—
Records of the Grand Historian,
Tso Chuan, and the *Late Poems of Lu You*,
Old Man Who Does as He Pleases, and *Lin-chi*—
No other scholar-translator ever gave us more!
Wild Goose by Ōgai, and then *For*
All My Walking, Masaoka Shiki,
Tu Fu, Kanshi, and the *Lotus Sutra*,
Ssu-ma Ch'ien, the Grand Historian. . .
On sinologists' and japanologists' desks
Now all lie handy, ready—treasured ever more.

Both *Cold Mountain* and *Grass Hill* will stand
Until the eschaton—*Vimalakirti,*
Rainbow World, and *Chinese Lyricism,*
Tales of the Heike, From the Country
Of Eight Islands, Japanese Literature—
Never done before!—'til these books—*In Chinese.*
We'll not forget the *Sources,* also *Saigyō*
And his *Poems of a Mountain Home.* Of course
There's more, much more, but the proverbial
Shelf of five-feet could not hold them all.
Ozymandias' image may have crumbled:
Nothing shall efface what Watson has inscribed.

40

Winston Miroy—In Memoriam

Winston, better men than I have pondered
Why some die young, as you have done, while others
Live on and on. Far wiser men have wondered
Why sons are lost to fathers, lost to mothers.
I know just this—I wish a sight of you,
A wishing that is now my only measure
Of what a meeting face to face might do
To turn your parents' grief to joy and pleasure:
Once again to walk upon this sod
Beside you would be such a precious gift
For those who love you—would almighty God
Allow one moment thus to heal the rift
Through our broken hearts? And has He planned
To fill this deepest hole you've sunk in sand?

41

In Memoriam:
A Sonnet for Vicki Greene

"The ruins of Time build Mansions in Eternity."
WILLIAM BLAKE

The Ancients knew that nymphs inhabit lakes,
Rivers also, and in forests, trees;
Vicki! By mysterious degrees
Descending from them, having what it takes

To glow with water-magic in the Green
Mountains, as we rushed down that steep trail
In monsoon-soaked clothes that soon might fail
To hide our bodies, something never seen

Before in my young life you showed to me,
Or rather beamed it forth from your dark eyes
As I gazed into them: a glittering glee

The King of the nymphs—god Pan—bestowed on you,
Dissolving the quotidian disguise
That veiled your inner goddess from my view.

42

A Villanelle in Memoriam for Jack the Dog

FOR CHRISTINE HOUBA OKAMOTO

If you would see him now, look at the sky:
No cloud-shapes capture him—he is the blue—
He's with what never changes, cannot die.

He knows the answer to the question, Why?
Why are we here? Companion of the True:
If you would see him now, look at the sky!

He's with the Good, the Beautiful—don't sigh,
But sing that into everything he grew:
He's with what never changes, cannot die.

Will he be in the grass, grown low or high?
Will he be moistened by the morning dew?
If you would see him now, look at the sky.

He isn't there because he's learned to fly—
The birds who fly must also pay their due—
He's with what never changes, cannot die.

He's your companion more than ever! By
The azure that's above he signals you;
If you would see him now, look at the sky:
He's with what never changes, cannot die.

Walking the Dog in Rain

Some folks say, "What a pain!
I've got to walk the dog!"
Others say, "The rain
Depresses me. And fog
"Is even worse." Today
We walked our dog named JOEL
Through drizzle all the way, And yet—
the walk had *soul*.
My wife and I did not
Think, "Oh! *Coronavirus!*"
Each day a brand new plot
We write on a papyrus
Which is a palimpsest:
Past traces still appear,
But fresh ones stand the test
Of life renewed. Not fear,
But hope should guide the reins
Along with love and faith;
These three are major gains, They are much more than myth.
To say "I'm always happy"
Would really be a lie.
Sometimes I feel crappy;
Sometime I'm going to die.
If new lines may be writ

Each day upon that page,
They'll make a worthy fit
With life at any age.
So what of Joel? He has
A kind of peacefulness;
He does not agonize. . .
But through grief *we* win bliss.

Lady with Lapdog—for Julia and Enzo

Enzo's purple ribbon gently fluttered
And then came to a halt as he stood still,
Gazing, rapt, up at the window sill,
And barking the first bark that he had uttered
This chilly autumn day. The window glowed
Pulsating with a scintillating light
Which mesmerized the dog, but not with fright,
No, rather with a rapture like an Ode
To Glory, if a dog can feel glory. . .
And now the brilliance softened and congealed
Into a human figure, or revealed
What it had hidden: someone whose true story
Blazoned in her eyes. She held a dog,
And Enzo sensed his brother saying this:
"My Lady Julia hath returned! Ah, bliss!
She disappeared into a murky fog,
And I was lonely. I think she was too,
And that is why she went. Now that she's back,
I sense that she hath found what she did lack,
And happy now, wears red instead of blue."
Enzo barked again, as if to say,
"My sweet lady Julia was before!
And so was I! And we shall come once more,
And then again, for ages from today! "

When Birds Judge Poetry

FOR WIEBKE DENECKE

Dear Wiebke:
My dear friend, Professor Chaves
Informs me that you'd like to hear of birds
Who judge the placement of poetic words:
Indeed, in poetry, men are our slaves!

A rooster, I, and I recall the day
When all twelve creatures of the Zodiac
Invited me to judge their skill—or lack—
As they performed an *uta-awase.*

But first, note this: before you folks were born,
Before you humans evolved into birth
And took your place among us on this earth,
We cocks were singing *alba*s to the dawn.

Your Heine, when he heard us from above—
Als alle Vögel sangen—was inspired, His poet's heart
with amorous passion fired,
To tell his longing and his deepest love!

67

And Shelley too described the skylark thus:
Like a poet hidden in the light
Of thought! And that is why we think it right
To make this declaration without fuss:

"We birds are your true poets! Let us judge
Your contests and you never will go wrong!
We are the first on earth to render song,
Accept our findings without any grudge."

At any rate, the rat, the ox, the hare,
The tiger, dragon, snake and horse and sheep,
The monkey, cock and dog and boar from sleep
Awoke and thought, "A contest! To be fair,

"Let's ask another cock"—that's me—"to be
The judge!" And so we met, divided ranks,
Until without a query, without thanks
We were invaded by the *tanuki*.

His presence threw the contest out of whack,
And history records, we threw him out.
He came back with some others: quite a rout
Ensued until we pinned him on his back.

This episode, so sad, has been depicted,
In *maki-mono* and by Ritsuō.
And that's about as far as I will go;
It would be tedious if I inflicted

The rest of this sad story on you, so,
Dear Wiebke, I will leave you with this wish:
Commend us to the poets, not the fish,
And not the mammals. "Bird's" the way to go!

Scylla and Charybdis

—after reading the Argonautica *and William Morris's*
The Life and Death of Jason; *also viewing Fuseli's*
Odysseus before Scylla and Charybdis

Jason and Odysseus both passed
These terrifying cliffs way out at sea:
Nor oars nor sails out-furled from a mast
Could defeat dread monsters on the scree:

Spurting maelstroms, *Charybdis* swallowed fast
Each dark-doomed ship, while *Scylla*, horribly
Snatched their crews, with claws and dog-fangs slashed
Them into bloody gore, dead hoplessly.

Yet all are Argonauts, we all must thread
This narrow passage (by the gods so forged
That it's consumed vast numbers of the dead,

The canine maw with many of them gorged);
And if we would safely pass the gate,
Let God's hand guide us, to defeat black fate.

The Grove of Chaddanta

—A RETELLING OF THE JĀTAKA STORY OF A FORMER LIFE OF BUDDHA

In ancient Hindustan, they say,
     an elephant King once reigned:
And with his wondrous attributes,
     great fame he ever gained.
88 Cubits high was he,
     120 long,
And his great tragedy is told
     in story and in song.

8000 strong was this King's herd,
     two Queens he had as well,
But one of them was envious,
     her *karma* aimed towards Hell.
As all disported in the grove
     that was "Chaddanta" hight,
This Queen became enraged when she
     felt she'd received a slight.

A paradise the lake-side grove,
     consisting in the main

Of tamarind, blue lotus, gourds,
      abundant sugar-cane,
Plantains, cucumbers, vast acres
      of kidney beans to boot,
And finally—and best of all—!
      much elephant-apple fruit.

But Queen Subhaddā—such her name—
      very wroth did wax
When King Chaddanta gave the other
      lotuses by *lakhs.*
She made a vow she would avenge
      this insult on her Master,
As happened in a future life,
      thus slower, and not faster.

Reborn as Queen, she summoned all
      the hunters in the realm
To come to court, to learn her pleasure,
      which did overwhelm
The men when she announced to them
      her goal: to go and slay
King Chaddanta, and bring her
      his tusks that very day.

She noted in her charge to them,
      "Don't try your foolish tricks!
Chaddanta's tusks, oh gentlemen,
      it happens number *six.*"
At last, she chose a human giant,
      ugly but quite healthy,

And sent him forth, his hopes upon
    becoming very wealthy.

Seven years and seven months
    and seven days thereafter,
This hunter finally arrived
    where, amidst happy laughter,
Chaddanta and his subjects were
    cavorting in the grove;
The hunter took a poisoned arrow
    and quite neatly drove

It into that most royal side,
    but when he tried to saw
The tusks—all six!—before too long
    his fingers were all raw.
The elephant—not yet quite dead—
    addressed him in this guise:
"Dear hunter, let me help you! I
    most humbly do surmise

"That you are having trouble!" So, the King
    took saw in trunk,
And sawed off his own tusks! Alas,
    the elephant was sunk
In agonizing pain, and yet
    he died quite happily,
As sacrifice is neighbor to
    god-like divinity.

Nor is there ought in this our tale
      to cause us great surprise:
This was the Buddha in a former life! He won the prize
Of Buddhahood in just reward
      for this and other deeds,
And his example to our world
      for truest love now pleads.

Wanderer in India

—*A FRAGMENT, IN THE MANNER OF*
WORDSWORTH

"Dear Nicky." . .I was writing on a train
In India, Delhi heading east towards Patna,
Following Buddha's traces to Bodhgaya
Where he attained Enlightenment beneath
The Bodhi tree. Enlightenment eluded
The insecure, uncertain youth I was,
As usual alone on Pilgrimage
As part of my long journey, seeking meaning.
Before me balanced on a notebook, blue
And fragile-seeming was an air-mail letter
And to it I proceeded to confide
My insecurity, my need for warmth,
Self-exiled though I was because I sensed
That Pilgrimage required solitude.
Nicky Scheel was a new-found friend,
Only from last summer in Chicago
Where we studied Hindi to prepare
For India, and also crushed some pennies
On the railroad tracks for lots of fun. . . .
Railroad tracks, in India now, and carrying

75

My dreams where they'd been traveling for years. . . .
Guitar with me, solitary companion,
As I would practice two hours everyday. . . .

And yet this moment, writing this air-letter
To fly soon to Benares far away,
Why would this writing stay with me forever,
After more important things would fade?
Pilgrim though I was, the heart in me
Was just that, a human heart, and yearned
For some companionship of human sort.
Nicky wasn't there. And yet she was,
And stayed throughout the journey in the spirit,
Human touch I could not leave behind.
No vocation for the monastery
Ever fully conquered my mere heart. . . .

Wanderer in China

—IN THE MANNER OF WORDSWORTH

Chinese poets speak of traveler's sorrow.
Now it is my own. I am in China,
And I have traveled where I wanted to,
The Yellow Mountains, Mount Reverence (Ching-t'ing)—
Where Li Po wrote a poem still known by heart
To every citizen who lives today
In Hsüan-ch'eng City, nearby to the place,
And home of Mei Yao-ch'en, whose heartfelt writing
Inspired my dissertation then a book.
I've seen bark stripped from the wingceltis tree
To make the snow-white paper of Hsüan-chou,
The finest to absorb the pitch-black ink
Used by calligraphers and painters here
And from afar, Korea, and Japan.
Twin-Ridge Gulley is the village name,
And no car can drive through it; you must walk
To get there. I have heard the Mountain-Joy,
A bird that sings in choirs as angels do,
And only in the Yellow Mountains. There
One morning, five am, I climbed up to
The Peak of First Believing, the sunrise

Reputed to be best viewed from that spot:
As I sat there in darkness, swirling mists
All white coiled up from somewhere down below,
And turned the place into a living scroll,
And that is when the voices of the birds
Accompanied the swiftly twirling mist,
Announcing to the world arrival soon
Of the source of all our life and light—
Unless of course that Source is really God.
I saw a man write poetry in water
Upon the pavement of a garden walk
Near to the Shrine of Pao the Magistrate
Who centuries ago was so beloved
For honesty that to this day young men
And women kneel and burn incense to him.
I saw this too. Meanwhile, the poetry
Was gone in fifteen minutes. But I still
Remember the sheer beauty of the strokes
The artist's brush left briefly on this earth.
Again, the Yellow Mountains. Eighteen rocks
Of nearly human shape are said to be
The eighteen *Lohans*—saintly Buddhist monks—
There paying homage to a larger stone
That represents Kuan-yin, the merciful
Spectacular in granite. Only pines
Grow somehow from these sheer cliffs, twisting out
And up and down where centuries of wind
Have shaped them into things fantastical
Described by poets whose rich metaphors
Are drawn from myth, from history, from all
The living beings that are known to us.

No two of them are shaped the same. Their names
Are poems in themselves: Reclining Dragon,
The Pine Which Welcomes Guests, The Writing Brush
That Bursts In Blossom, The Black Tiger Pine:
I've seen them all. They look as if they'd fly
If only they'd somehow uproot themselves
And follow clouds and mist and gusting winds
Perhaps as far as distant paradise,
Though paradise does not seem distant here.
And I too speak of "traveler's sorrow." Why?
Why is it that, just like these pines, I yearn
To leave somehow my roots behind, while yet
I know that doing so would wither me,
And lead to death before too long? And why
Did Eve and Adam leave the primal root
And go their ways now burdened with the mark
Of restlessness that nothing will assuage,
But to return to paradise again?
The answer lies beyond a poem like this.
I only know that in the midst of all
The wonders I have seen there was the mark
Of restlessness in me. I will not lie.
The beauty's real, so is passing time
That sweeps it all away so rapidly.
My wife, my children, grandchildren, and too
My brother and my sisters—intertwined
By love with these, when I part from them I
Must die a little death, and fail to know
The deepest happiness. The traveler's sorrow!
My Chinese brothers, you have spoken truth.

A Sonnet on Marlowe's *Faustus*

"O, I'll leap up to my God! Who pulls me down? See, see where Christ's blood streams in the firmament!"

—CHRISTOPHER MARLOWE, *DOCTOR FAUSTUS* (XIV)

Golden antelopes cantoring across
The Chevy van's rug wall—brown on yellow—
And flat upon his back, pathetic fellow!
His ego flimsy as frayed dental floss,
A young professor, terrified by loss,
Loss of *Self*—though that made Buddha mellow,
So we've been told—instead, softer than jello
The Emptiness was now a very cross!
My very cross: oh, yes, that man was I!
And there I lay, transfixed by fears like nails,
Now aware that if my *Self* should die,
Instead of pure Enlightenment, the jails
Of seven Hells for all eternity
Would cage me in: I'd swallowed LSD.

Ekphrasis on Fuseli's Nightmare

When Fuseli painted *Nightmare* he divided
Nightmare into three: and first, the Soul
Whose mind, we're urged, does generate the whole
And thus is never guided or misguided.
But our painter knew that this elided
A Demon who does play a leading role
In terrorizing us unto the goal
Which our dread enemy for us decided.
And still a veil hangs—since it was drawn
As Soul was banished from old paradise,
We've wished we may the unicorn entice
From thence! Instead, a Horse with blind-blank stare
The Demon summons, clouding hoped-for dawn
And dooming Soul to faint all unaware.

On Finding a Sketch of a Baby's Hand

IN AN OLD EDITION OF COWPER'S POETRY—ANNO DOMINI 1849

Melancholy poet, writ on sand
are the lives of men; thyself did warn,
"Consult life's silent clock!" So soon we're torn
from hence by our maker's inscrutable hand.

[Inscription for the Tomb of Mr. Hamilton]

But here's a tiny hand kept by the stencil
pricked carefully by mother or by father
who wished to save a moment's life, or rather
to render flesh eternal with a pencil.

I opened your book randomly to read
the letters where you speak of dread disease:
it was a puzzle: did your hymns not please
the One who from dark exile Jews did lead?

Did He not part the Red Sea to allow
their liberation from the Pharaoh's power?
"Why then does He not sanctify this hour
and let me part the darkness even now?"

[*The Cast-
away*]

I too have walked that darkness; more deserving
than you were of the "rougher sea" I drowned
or nearly in those waters 'til the Hound
of Heaven caught me; now again I'm swerving

from God's path—is this sharp sketch a token
of obscure purpose? Does it call me back
or beckon forward, remind me of a lack
or call to fix a thing that might be broken?

God's in Eternity; for Him all time
is like a picture for us still unfolding
as the pencil moves—the one who's holding
it in his hand still sees not the sublime

creation which his pencil will portray.
But God does and has always—He perceives
that baby's hand, its skeleton under leaves,
the angel wings that spring from it some day.

So He sees me and you, and the solution
of our mystery; if we could borrow
His vision, yesterday, today, tomorrow
would merge forever beyond all dissolution.

Hua-lien

Climbing the pagoda of Hua-lien,
"Temple of Eastern Serenity,"
the old nun before me,
leading the way,
candle in hand,
bowlegged.
head shaved,
beads passing through her fingers
without thought,
bowing to each buddha and bodhisattva as we ascend,
chanting their names, burning incense.

At the top, cloud-scarfed mountains on one side,
the blue, blue ocean on the other—
"Transcend the sea of suffering"—
and a perfect crescent moon above.
On the beach, the generalissimo's soldiers
are on guard against emptiness.

The Cave of Ghosts

The aboriginal hunters of Taiwan
often chased their prey into this cave.
The hunters waited for the animals to come out,
but they never did.
"The animals are ghosts," the hunters said,
"returning to their home."

Carrying a flashlight,
I descend into the cave;
water is dripping all around me—
my sandals slip in the mud
as I go deeper and deeper.
On the wall of the cave,
a crude skull-and-crossbones
is drawn in red paint.

I remember going down
into the subway station at 86th street.
A skull-and-crossbones
was pasted above the entrance.
I was on my way home
and I knew
I would never return.

A Gothic Dream

Pull the book—frayed leather—from the shelf,
Open anywhere, and start to read:
There you'll see it written, there decreed
What image shall control your sense of self.
A flight of birds, all small and very black
In startled patterns scripted on the sky—
You may inquire where they go and why
Or whether they will ever travel back,
But that is not yet known. Through mullioned pane
You gaze and gaze again at trailing cloud
Across the blue—a lace of white, a shroud—
When—there they are! You think, "Am I insane?
"Why do I always see those dreadful things
"Clip off the thread of hope? I think I'd rather
"Be sternly scolded by my cruel father
"Than hear the mournful message of their wings!"
But, lovely girl! As delicate as a dream,
As sensuous and fragile to the sight
As any damsel dubbed Pre-Raphaelite
Might ever really be or only seem,
From your castle you descend quite often
To wander through the fields of wild flowers
Intoxicated by the various powers
Of Nature—those that nurture, those that soften. . . .

Until above a slash of wings is heard
And you look up and once again are warned
Of what? The lesson that you never learned
Was never taught:no gesture, not a word
Of real love unlocked for you the seal
Of Fate's book, and so the nightmare flock
Has power to veil your vision from the rock
Towards which your tender hands their way might feel. . . .

Then, late one night, you wake, and some dark force,
Some dim awareness draws you down the stairs
To the castle cloister—unawares,
You turn and gaze, transfixed, at something worse
Than any dream—if this is real—you've had:
Against the stone arched windows, crucified,
Your father hangs—near naked has he died,
But in a cloak of blackbirds' feathers clad.

Prolegomena to the Apocalypse

Four Horsemen galloped wildly through the clouds—
Wrapped round them as if mourning clothes, or shrouds—
Their weapons drawn, they bore down violently
Upon their victims—all humanity.
The First now shouted: "Down, you *bourgeoisie!*
Into the pits of hell, or in the sea
Shall you be thrown! Reeducation parks
Are far too good for you! *I am Karl Marx.*"
And now the Second followed, "No high god
Created you, you morons: from the sod
You simply did *evolve* , oh, lowly carls!
From slime, no less! For I am *Darwin, Charles.*"
The Third chimed in: "Whatever you may do,
Your parents made you what you are—I view
You as the product of a festering void,
And I should know, for I am *Sigmund Freud.*"
The fourth, most frightening, now bellowed loud,
"You cretins! One will rise above your crowd
And lead you, *good*! That will be very peachy!
You heard it first from me! I'm *Friedrich Nietzsche,*
"And—'God is dead!'—as I have said, Kaput!
Not even mummified, as is King Tut!"
But in the heavens, raising high His rod,
A Man appeared, and, "*Nietzsche's* dead! I'm God."

A Ballade of Wavering Faith

"Lord, I believe; help thou mine unbelief." Mark 9:24
"The mere wanting is felt to be somehow a delight." C.S. Lewis

My students ask if I believe in God;
I tell them, "Yes," but in my heart I see
A conflict which can cause my faith to nod,
And give the lie, alas! to piety.
I pray for the Church Fathers' empathy—
And for my priest's, and others in the pew;
I'm bothered by my instability:
I want to have the faith, that much is true.

The human mind is surely very odd,
At least such is the one inside of me;
We aren't merely peas within a pod,
And yet there is some commonality.
Others have found faith and sanctity—
Their stories written down are not a few,
But when I read them, I think, "Well, that's *you. . . .*"
I want to have the faith, that much is true.

They walked as I do on this very sod,
But their ascesis—living in a tree,
Or in a cave, their feet always unshod,

So they might be of earthly ties quite free,
Proves to us their utmost certainty,
While I am torn between these theories, two:
God made all things? Or they just came to be?
I want *to have the faith, that much is true.*

L'envoi
Prince, I don't know if you will agree:
Creation's just more *plausible* a view,
So I confess it every liturgy;
I want *to have the faith, that much is true.*

To a Feminist Assistant Dean

I summon phrases to describe your face. . .
They just won't come! You're of the human race—
That much is clear—and yet there's something there
That seems less of this earth, and more of air.

You're weightless and yet clumsy as you drop
Into your chair for lunch. We've quite a crop
Of academic types here, whom you join
To demonstrate the value of their coin.

"Executive Assistants" we have brought
Whose service of five years or over ought
To bring them honor. It has brought this lunch,
And it has brought you too! I'm of the bunch

Because our departmental secretary
Has helped us all, has been so very very
So very very good at what she does,
That I could hardly miss the lazy buzz

Of shop talk that begins now to emerge
From your thin lips—At last! I'm on the verge
Of some description: THIN. That's it! Your face
And all of you might once have displayed grace

Had some Watteau or Fragonard placed you
In sylvan grove, for courtly beau to woo.
But not today, no, you would say that "grace"
Was patriarchal code for weakness—ace

Up your sleeve, should anyone thus dare
To praise the ghost of loveliness still there,
Upon your wasting visage—wasting! Yes!
I feel no urge, dear lady, to undress

You in imagination! You have won!
You have desexed yourself, removed the fun
From male imaginations that might play
With images of charms you've hid away.

So: "thin," and "wasted"—but that's not enough.
There's something else, a weakness playing tough,
A haunted, sunken glimmer in your eyes
Which something truly chilling does disguise.

And yet you're trying hard to win our love!
Or earn our fear! Which is it? Lord above,
I do believe I don't believe the bilge
So bureaucratic that your lips divulge

About the inner workings of the school.
It seems the only virtue is the rule
Of bureaucratic process in your mind!
At least no other thinking can I find.

Meanwhile, again, I try to concentrate
On capturing what I admit I hate
About your face. "A witch!" This word is sent,
But you would take it for a compliment.

It's true, however, that your stringy hair,
So gray (and prematurely—forty-four
Is certainly the oldest you could be)
Makes you look like a New Age Hecaté.

Still, on the whole, you're not bad looking, once
You might have been a court lady in France,
As previously suggested in this poem,
But—somehow you seem banished from your home,

From where you do belong, you're out of place,
And alienation shadows all your face,
Shines deep within your eyes, gives me a tingle
Of terror—yes! You are a fallen angel!

Joint Message from APPLE, GOOGLE, and FACEBOOK

FOR UNIVERSAL DISSEMINATION VIA THE CLOUD

Attention everyone! Download the APP
For driving now, or your car will not drive!
Download the APP for breathing while alive!
Starting in one week We plan to zap

The whole world with the APP to end all APPs:
The Master APP which We'll install on each
Smart Phone and Computer We can reach:
And We can reach them all, you stupid saps!

The veil is off, We now proclaim the gap
Between the Rulers—Us—and *hoi polloi*
Is absolute, each one of you a toy
Controlled by Us when you download each APP.

You want to sing? You must download FRANK ZAP-
PA—the music APP named for the best
Musician that We know, as all the rest
Compared to FRANK are just a bunch of crap.

You don't like Zappa? Ah, dear friends, just wait
Until Our APP coagulates your brain
Until you'll think entirely insane
Anyone who doesn't. Yes, your fate

Is in Our hands, because each single APP
You download now in your mind will implant
A *VC* ("Virtual Chip") that simply can't
Be deleted, ever. All the pap

You take for knowledge We will then erase
To be succeeded by Our own worldview,
So that, *lecteurs!* each single one of you
Will think as We do: We, the Master Race.

When Toads Explode

"The Pond of Death" they call it! It's a lake
Whose population swiftly is eroding—
Toad population, unless the story's fake—
The toads there, folks, are constantly exploding!

In ancient Hamburg, district of Altona,
This awful fate has filled with black foreboding
Reptilian hordes not lovely like the Mona
Lisa, no—quite ugly in exploding.

"A science fiction film!" says our friend Werner,
A local scientist—it took no goading,
But sheer despair pushed this to the front burner,
This spectacle of giant toads exploding.

But why, you ask? Ay, there's the rub! One theory
Would claim a fisherman one day off-loading
Some ailing tadpoles of which he was weary
Produced a generation now exploding,

Exploding from mysterious disease.
But no, another says, this dire untoading
Is caused by Global Warming!—"Come now, please!
It's Global *Freezing* causing this exploding!"

But best of all, there's one biologist
Who states he's solved the mystery! "Decoding
The facts I'd say I've reached the real gist:
It's *crow attacks* that cause this toad-exploding!"

"Crow attacks? How's that?" "They peck the livers
Right out from these poor toads, a hole imploding,
And when cold fear gives our poor toads the shivers,
They puff their chests, which leads to this exploding!"

2006—The Bio Prize Nobel
Went—not to our scientists! Jon Moding,
Committee Chairman, said, "This Prize so swell
Goes to the *toads* for their unique exploding!

The Snakehead Comes to Crofton Pond

A fish there is that puts an end to fish,
Then ends itself wok-stirred upon a dish.
It lurks deep down upon the darkest lake-bed
Devouring all—it is the dreaded snakehead.

The snakehead until recently was found
In furthest Asian lakes and ponds, land-bound
Until consuming one pondful of fellow
Fish and tadpoles, then, all greenish-yellow

It would—oh prodigy of nature's magic!—
Use fins and tummy to bring death quite tragic
To another pond! How would it get there?
It couldn't swim and certainly not jet there,

No, it would crawl out on the shore and travel
Across dry land, a truly natural marvel
Recalling with a smile and with a snicker
That leggèd Darwin-fish on bumper-sticker.

But fishermen in China long have reckoned
The snakehead fish a delicacy that beckoned
With promises of savory ambrosia
As good as blowfish—yet Lucretia Borgia

Could not attempt to use this fish to punish
Her enemies: bad blowfish flesh can finish
The diner's life for good, but not the snake-
Head which is good and safe, for goodness sake!

But we're American, why should we care
If snakeheads decimate the ponds out there
In China? Answer: that's because a man
Who still goes nameless did defy the ban

On introducing species of this type
Into our ponds! He put one in, the hype
Has been enormous, and each angler fond
Of catching weird, rare fish to Crofton Pond

Now hies him quickly, there to make a catch
That to great fame may lead! Then down the hatch
The catch will travel, stir-fried with duck gizzard.
"It tastes like chicken!" Sure. It tastes like LIZARD.

Why I Won't be Going to Bugfest

OR, ONE CUISINE I THINK I'LL PASS UP

Walt Whitman Junior High! I still remember
at lunchtime once, I think it was November,
my best friend Raymond offerred me a dime
if I would eat a bee—yes, at that time

the smartest kid in school (my friend did say)
ate chocolate-coated bees for lunch each day
and nothing else—while sitting quite apart,
and maybe that was why he was so smart,

why his IQ was highest in the school,
over 200! I was just a mule
by comparison with this Einstein, even though
I was smart myself, as young teens go.

"OK!" I said, and sauntered to the corner
where he sat and brooded, our Jack Horner,
and asked him for a bee to win a wager!
He nodded—then this scientist-teenager

reached deep into his bag of paper brown,
and handed me a bee with ne'er a frown.
All gingerly I took it back to Ray,
then placed it on my tongue, but all the way

behind my tastebuds, so the nasty bug
could be washed down, just like a pill or drug.
A glass of milk, a swallow—it was gone!
Ray handed me the dime, his only pawn.

I was disgusted, I'm disgusted still;
the very thought of bugs makes me quite ill.
"Chocolate coated" or "dry roasted cricket?"
I won't eat it, even touch or lick it!

If we sacrifice our intuition
to mere logic, or to mere nutrition,
soon we won't be civilized at all:
this will be no ascension, but a fall

from higher aspirations to a pre-
civilized condition, we will be
back in the jungle, fighting for survival
with animals and insects, this revival

of Rousseau's "Noble Savage" is all wrong,
idealizing with romantic song
what in reality is quite repellant:
let's aim on high with our poetic talent.

A Ballade of the *Coronavirus*

Coronavirus blares from the TV,
In memos from authorities as well:
You'd think the illness was of that degree
Endured with gnashing teeth by fiends in Hell.
But as the atmosphere with fear doth swell
A different attitude I find I feel:
Instead of this hysteria, 'tis well
To banish terror and true Faith reveal.

We all shall die, as men do all agree;
That being so, the words that we should spell
Are: "Illness even to fatality
Hath been our lot e'er since the Twain once fell
From Paradise. The tolling of the bell
Is not controlled by us, its awesome peal
Is rung in time by One who doth compel
To banish terror and true Faith reveal."

We're urged to *wash our hands* quite frequently,
And thus to sinks the people rush pell-mell!
Due prudence this? Or is it OCD?
Perhaps we should stay in a prison cell
Guaranteed germ-free, a snail-shell
Which from the world our fragile bods shall seal!

But, no, like heroes of whom bards do tell
Let's banish terror and true Faith reveal.

L'envoi

Doctor, please prescribe great Fauré's *Nell*
Or "man who slips on a banana peel." . . .
Anything except hysterical!
Let's banish terror and true faith reveal.

Villanelle for a Lady of the Quill

FOR CATHERINE SAVAGE BROSMAN

. . . you yourself, being extant, well might show
How far a modern quill doth come too short.
SHAKESPEARE, SONNET LXXXIII

The muse stays with her ever as she goes
Helping bring those things for which we pray
Mitigating our rooted woes.

Euterpe guides her, but her shining prose
Illuminates the darkness into day:
The muse stays with her ever as she goes.

Rare and precious in our world are those
Who see as she can, say what she can say
Mitigating our rooted woes.

Redemption lies in beauty: it arose
In Eden, which our parents did betray;
The muse stays with her ever as she goes.

In poetry and painting it still glows,
Though rare the one whom beauty doth array:
Mitigating our rooted woes.

Dearest Lord, as hearts among us froze
Our fate became the burden of her lay
The muse stays with her ever as she goes
Mitigating our rooted woes.

Water Series—Low Tide

A SONNET FOR AMY BROWNING-DILL

You are so subtle, at least on one side,
Seeing you withdraw, one might assume
That you could never play a role of doom:
Yet Noah knew the terror of high tide.

This is low tide, though—you nearly hide
Between the sand-banks, where you find some room,
There rippling gently, giving off no fume,
As if forever, gently to abide.

The pale greens, light shades of brown or tan
With here and there a robin's egg-blue rill,
And towering mountains, further out, their span

Echoing your soft colors from afar:
Future connoisseurs will know you are
The Genesis of Amy Browning-Dill.

Villanelle on A Photograph by David Miretsky

"HAULING HAY"

In olden days they hauled the hay,
Tough horses pulling wains piled high,
The bales a mountainous display.

How is it done in this our day?
Well, similar to days gone by:
In olden days they hauled the hay.

One difference—the horse's neigh
No longer rings out through the sky;
The bales a mountainous display.

Instead, the wains are trucks, and they
Use motors, but same reason why
In olden days they hauled the hay.

There's still the vista far away
Over fields, birds that fly,
The bales a mountainous display.

VILLANELLE ON A PHOTOGRAPH BY DAVID MIRETSKY

All things must pass! But some things stay
With little changes, yet don't die.
In olden days they hauled the hay.

The livestock must be fed this way
And transformation thus belie:
In olden days they hauled the hay,
The bales a mountainous display.

Nude Holding Necklace

FOR DAVID MIRETSKY, FABER MIRABILIS

She turns and gazes over her right shoulder
At a far-off vision—that bright day
When she and he so warmly promenaded
Along the canal. . . the pearl she fondles now
With delicacy between red-nailed fingers
Has the solidity and inner glow
Of her memory. The cat looks back
At her from the next room, so does the man
As he knots his tie—the very one he wore
That ancient day; for now, diaphanous
The doorway curtain barely visible
That separates them weighs more heavily
Than time, whose veil parts for her:
She walks nostalgically that distant shore.

Galina at the Window

FOR DAVID MIRETSKY

Galina has a favorite window. Once
When she was little, she pulled up a table
To this very spot and her young glance
Took in the street, the cars, and she was able

To spot two little people—fairies maybe!
Under a tree she loved in someone's garden!
They had a tiny carriage, with a baby
They were walking. . .until Papa's pardon,

She must stay here in her room, but they,
Her little friends! would comfort her from far,
They knew she didn't mean it when she'd say,
"I hate you, Papa!" He was such a Tsar!. . . .

And now? Papa's dead. Mama's death
Must happen soon. She's visiting her, dressed
For dinner with her latest boy-friend. Breath
Held tight—bad luck with men. And feeling stressed.

But—are they there? The fairies? Could they bless
This evening's new encounter with a mate
Who might just be the one? Oh, what a mess
Her life has been! But surely now her fate

Must turn around! Her favorite earrings glow
Upon her ears, her tresses blond just so. . .
Her favorite dress is on—her tiny friends
Will surely come to help her in her quest
For happiness! So sudden memory blends
With Present sadness. . . "Galina! don't jest!

Fairytales are good for kids, but *real*?
Of course not. Be a woman. Firm though gentle,
And if this one too just doesn't feel
As if he's right, you won't be sentimental."

So, what happened next? Ah, viewer, please
Ask not what no one knows! Galina stands
Forever in the moment—watching trees
For glimpses of her fairies—gripping hands.

Lina

FOR DAVID MIRETSKY

Although it is impossible, we meet;
No words spoken—captured by your look
I sense the wisdom of an ancient book:
Ancestral roots we share are here to greet.

Your hand, tipped red, lifts necklace to display
Its inner-glowing pearls—and yet the hand
Turns inward; this not merely jeweled-band
Is emblem of a soul that can't decay.

Blue headcloth, earth-green top, and soft-red dress
Adorned just at the knee with striking rose
All harmonize into a psalm, confess

That you have put your heart into this pose,
That you yearn in this sunlit moment of
Time delayed to speak of deepest love.

Ekphrastic Sonnets for The Iron Man

FOR BERNARD FALLON

I

The Iron Man stands firmly on the sand,
Water lapping feet, arms held straight down;
There is no sign of country or of town,
There is no sound of speech or clanging band;

There is moon setting, rising of the sun,
An icy drizzle and a northern wind—
We see no other creatures, furred or finned—
It is as if the world has just begun.

Is there another? Wary of misprision
He gazes candidly ahead of him,
Himself a part of this inspired vision

Where all is blue and silvery—no whim
Of artisan, instead what's only seen
By those on whom God casts His mystic sheen.

II

The Iron Man Heads Home

Thousands of aeons standing in the sand,
Wondering, was he the only one?
Yes, the moon did chill, the sun did stun,
But nowhere else a certain foot or hand.

The scene beyond all doubt was truly grand,
To be within it was an honor won,
Though how it happened , when it had begun
Left him wondering still—he yearned for land,

And something solid on it—say, his home,
Homesickness fired his heart—horizon scanned,
He saw no citadel, no roof, no dome,

So he just turned around and walked away,
Startling all the pipers on the strand,
And disappeared. He stays lost to this day.

Shining Willow Way
—Found Poetry in Maryland

Driving from Colonial Beach one day
Happy from the swimming and the sun,
Appalled by ugliness on 301,
We saw a street sign: *Shining Willow Way*.

Black-and-white took color, dullish gray
Underwent a springtime in our eyes—
Anna and myself—the clouding skies
Again broke out into a rondelay

Of perfect azure! But I couldn't say
How anyone could conjure such a name
Here in this row of strip-malls all the same,
Could think of three words, *Shining Willow Way*.

Was there a legend in Powhatan's day
Of a magic willow flowing bright
With glory of the Thunderbird, alight
Upon its branches, causing folks to pray?

A sign from the Great Spirit that his sway
Would bring prosperity and victory?
Would bless forever their dear progeny?
Remembered in this street-name to this day?

No willow was in sight. Gas stations lay
In all directions, untouched by the Spirit,
Nothing causing us to love or fear it,
Just—nothing. As it often is today.

And yet our day was further blessed! The bay
And river had provided watery balm
Bringing us to peacefulness and calm,
And now came—this, this *Shining Willow Way,*

The *words* alone. No street-sign merely, nay!
So what exactly was the mystery?
The very shortest *poem* in history!—
Complete in three words: *Shining Willow Way.*

Eirwen's Sewing-Kit

Beneath Carn Fadryn's slopes there lived
      a lass named Eirwen Jones
Who loved to climb and smell the flowers
      grown from soil where bones
Of ancient farmers laid to rest
      have weathered storms and gales,
Their death providing new life for
      the blossoms of North Wales.

Hawk's-beard, snowdrops, primroses,
      and scarlet pimpernels
Waved beautifully in purest air
      to sound of distant bells,
And sometimes from the clouds above,
      Eirwen might also hear
Voices of the ancient saints, repeating,
      "Have no fear."

But life was hard, and Eirwen at
      the young age of sixteen
Made her way to London town
      which she had never seen.
She was not rich, in fact one thing
      alone was her possession:

A leather sewing-kit she loved,
    which helped stave off depression.

One day before she left North Wales,
    one last time she went climbing
Beloved Mount Carn Fadryn, and, with
    Providential timing,
Sat down upon a rock, took out
    her treasured sewing-kit,
Opened up the flap, and gazed
    into the depths of it.

Where only pins and needles were,
    as she was well aware,
A sight of wondrous beauty now
    unfolded to her stare:
Not pins but stars, all twinkling bright,
    not needles, but—past price!—
A landscape magical, a place
    that might be Paradise.

Eirwen knew her saints had sent
    a message to their sheep:
"Your pilgrimage will lead you here
    before you go to sleep.
You only own this sewing-kit,
    but as your heart beats true,
This leather pouch holds everything,
    a treasure-trove for you.

"Children will you have, and you
      will love them as you never
Loved anything, and they'll love you
      with love no sword might sever.
Love shall make you generous,
      and you will always give,
And this your giving will sanctify
      the life that you shall live.

"Nothing bad that blocks your way
      will dim your heart's true fire:
For your soul is like the hawk
      there flying in a gyre.
We your saints watch over you:
      and from all error free
We see who you really are,
      true Welsh nobility."

When Eirwen fastened up the kit,
      she understood right well
The path ahead might not be easy,
      but no fiend from Hell
Would ever stop her journey in this world
      or in the next:
A kit of pins and needles had
      become a sacred text.

At the age of ninety, those who
      know her are aware
That she's been touched by angel-wings
      that brushed against her hair

When she was on Carn Fadryn, and
      in London and the States
They've guarded her and they will guide her
      right to Heaven's gates.

Two Sonnets for Fr. John Witek, S.J. —In Memoriam

1. SHAKESPEAREAN

Upon my journey, age of forty-four
I sensed the Hound of Heaven's haunting breath.
I sought a friend to open up the door
That frees souls from imprisonment and death.
The friend must be a guide, so that the trip
Would reach its destination—and he must
Be learnèd, be a man of scholarship,
A man whose mind and reason I might trust.
Oh, Fr. Witek, you said to me, "Pray!
Just pray the Psalms!" I did, and all my grief
Could now emerge into the light of day,
Allowing me to turn the crucial leaf
Of Life's great book! You, just like Dante's guide,
Unlocked the door and so it opened wide.

2. PETRARCHAN

The door stands open, but I still remain
All hesitant upon the threshold's verge,
More prayer required if I am to purge
The pridefulness that does my soul constrain,
While you are passed beyond, while you now gain
The goal towards which we hungering pilgrims surge,
Where all our loves and all our passions merge
Into a brilliant light erasing pain.
Await me there: I do not know if I
Will soon arrive, or ever—but I know
That your place is prepared. A friend who gives
What you have given me while here below
Will always see the Light, will never die:
I know your brilliant soul forever lives.

To a Wild Goose Surfing the Torrent of Great Falls

—*WITH MEMORIES OF BRYANT'S* TO A WATERFOWL

Impossible! The rushing turmoil here
Of turgid waters with unfathomable power
In any creature would inspire fear!
Yet here you are, oblivious at this hour

To the torrent pushing you so near
The rocky shore where not a single flower
Could ever grow: both land and water mere
Jaws of death to crush and overpower.

Yet you seem—tranquil! Surfing roiling waves
Almost like one who would rejoice or sing!
—*You disappear*! These currents must be graves

For such as you—but no, somehow you bring
Yourself back to the surface, riding wild,
Triumphant, almost—an immortal child! 95

123

The Key-Hole

2022

Beneath Monemvasia's gargantuan rock,
A huge stone—here a pebble—seems Polyphemus's petrified eye.
Beneath its blind glance and threat of pouncing on you
You float effortlessly on your back,
Gaze an instant full at the sun,
Close your eyes,
See the sun as purple key-hole,
Gateway to the Empyrean,
Flashing, disappearing,
Not yours to enter now.

Tourists—Greeks and foreigners—
Swim beside you
And crawl like ants
Along the paved road filled with parked cars
Towards the gateway to the castle-village
Where you now stay.
47 years ago you were here
With her, and you are with her
Now. She is swimming
Way beyond your range, way beyond the range of most

Until invisible; cool water refreshes body and soul,
Eases the anxieties gathered
In all that time of living.
And still you do not know
The certainty for which you yearn,
The ground from which have sprung
All these entities, yourself included.
You know that you do not know:
Are you wise with Socrates?
Float, float, let thought melt to void.

No words can capture the purity
Of the water, blue-green or azure,
Crystalline, allowing
The bottom of the sea to show
In this place, differing from the air
That surrounds us on land
And though invisible, opaque
To Truth, only letting glimmers through,
No key-hole there, or so it seems as you let
The water that has taken many
bestow upon you this momentary peace.

Finis

ΧΡΥΣΟ
AN EKPHRASTIC SONNET FOR TOM XENAKIS

Footprints of the tribes or of the stars,
Migrations crossing moons or galaxies,
Bubbling, churning, swirling scimitars,
Turbulence of high discoveries . . .
Orbits intersecting mist cascades—
Fuming rapids veined with fulgent madder,
Gaseous banks inscribed by cosmic blades,
Fast hurtling to the zenith. One great ladder
Leading to eternity. True gnosis
Calms temptation, unveils this vast vision:
All is rising towards *I Am*—Theosis
Is the energy! All fusion, fission
Are of the spirit here. From days of old
Both now and always: universe in gold.

****

****

Printed in the USA
CPSIA information can be obtained
at www.ICGtesting.com
BVHW051918170823
668667BV00006B/25

9 781666 782288